LESSONS DOGS TEACH US

LESSONS
DOGS
TEACH US

Owning and Training a Dog: What We
Learn about Life, Love, and Loyalty

Cindy A. Rose

XULON PRESS

Xulon Press
2301 Lucien Way #415
Maitland, FL 32751
407.339.4217
www.xulonpress.com

Unless otherwise indicated, Scripture quotations are taken from the Holy Bible, New International Version Copyright 1973, 1978, 1984, 2011 by Biblica, Inc.

Photo on front cover by Phyllis Ensley

Paperback ISBN-13: 978-1-66281-279-8
Hardcover ISBN-13: 978-1-66281-280-4
Ebook ISBN-13: 978-1-66281-281-1

TABLE OF CONTENTS

INTRODUCTION

Dogs bring much joy and companionship to us; we can, in turn, learn a lot from our dogs. They teach us to live in the present and how to love each other. Most importantly, our canine companions can teach us about God's love for us.

I have owned several types of dogs over my lifetime. My first was a black Labrador Retriever named Jet that my parents bought for me at the age of ten. On my own, I trained Jet to heel, sit, lie down, stay, and come; I even showed him in Junior Showmanship. I had a Keeshond named Windy as a teenager who I also showed in Junior Showmanship. We had other family dogs over the years also including Fluffy, who was a mixed breed we got from the local pound, and Jill, a Shetland Sheepdog when I was in college.

As an adult, I have owned four Shetland sheepdogs (shelties), two of whom my husband and I still have. We have also had, or still have, an Aussie/Lab mix, two Australian Shepherds, two Australian Cattle Dogs, a Cattle Dog/Border Collie mix, a rescue Cocker Spaniel, and two Belgian Shepherds.

I have shown all the shelties in obedience and/or rally obedience and three of them in agility. I have shown both the Aussies in agility, although they were primarily handled by my husband. I also trained the Cocker for agility and then let my husband show him. Both of my Belgians, who have excelled in rally and agility, have taught me a lot as a dog owner/trainer/handler. I have learned different things from all my dogs. My husband and I have also owned and operated a small dog boarding kennel for the past eighteen years. We also teach other people how to train their dogs for basic obedience and/or agility.

God, my Father, has used the dogs I've owned or worked with over my lifetime to help me understand His love for me and what my relationship with Him looks like. I hope the examples in this book will help you to have a better understanding of God's love as well.

Part 1

LESSONS TAUGHT BY ALL TYPES OF DOGS

1
DEPENDENCE/MASTER

Dogs, especially young puppies, are totally dependent on their owners. The owner/master provides his or her dog with food, water, shelter, and love. A dog cannot go to the store and buy its own food. It cannot go to a pet store and buy a new toy. Unfortunately, some dogs do not get as much attention and care as they need. These dogs may look to their own devices to find something in the house to eat, such as books, furniture, shoes, etc. Or, they may try to make up their own games of chasing the neighbors or the neighbor's cat. But in an optimal situation, a dog owner will provide everything the dog needs, including training him or her to do what the owner wants, or training the dog not to do what the owner does not want him or her to do. Dogs who are usually the happiest are those whose owners not only provide their physical needs, such as food, water, and shelter, but they also give them adequate training, discipline, and love.

Likewise, people are dependent on God; He created us. Psalm 139:13 says, *"For you created my inmost being; you knit me together in my mother's womb. I praise you because I am fearfully and wonderfully made; your works are wonderful; I know that full well."* God provides us with everything we need. Some people may choose to reject God, but that does not mean He does not affect their lives. He provides us with the intelligence to get an education and a job. They may go to work and think they have achieved everything on their own, but God gave them the ability to do that job or achieve those goals. God, our Father, also gives us people who love us. He created us and He loves us.

Sometimes our dogs may become sick or seriously injured. At these times, they are completely dependent on us. We take them to the vet, administer their medications, nurse their wounds, and reinforce how much we love them.

People also sometimes become ill. We are wise to seek medical care when appropriate. However, at these times, we can also look to God for His healing power and comfort. He will often provide family members or friends to take care of our needs.

It can sometimes be difficult for us to depend on God. We may think, "I'm in control" or "I can do this." But the Bible tells us in Proverbs 3:5-6, *"Trust in the Lord with all your heart and lean not on your own understanding; in all your ways submit to Him and He will make your paths straight."* It also tells us in Hebrews 11:6, *"And without faith it is impossible to please God,* because anyone who comes to Him must believe that He exists and that He rewards those who earnestly seek him."

Dog owners often refer to themselves as "master." When we are good to our dog, providing for every physical need as well as playing with him or her and training him or her to do what we want, the dog's life will likely revolve around us. The pup may be momentarily distracted by something else, but ultimately his or her total devotion is to us. He or she wants to be with us all the time.

My sheltie, Jesse, likes to play with toys, run around the yard, and play with other dogs. But more than anything, he wants to be near me and interact with me. This is exactly how God wants our relationship with Him to be. Well, okay, He may not care if we like to play with toys or run around the yard. But we likely have other things we enjoy, such as sports, shopping, or watching television. It is okay to enjoy God's gifts to us. It is okay to enjoy activities, such as golf, cooking, knitting, hiking, etc., but our major focus should be on God. He should be our Master. He loves for us to spend time with Him in Bible study and prayer.

When I used to work as a pharmacist, I would usually be gone for ten or more hours a day. When I returned home, my dogs were very excited to see me. God does not go away and leave us, but sometimes we may forget that He is with us. We can learn from our dogs, because we should be just as excited about spending time with Jesus in Bible study and prayer as a dog is about seeing its owner. And when we have the opportunity to go to worship service on Sunday morning, it is something to be excited about – to go and worship our Lord. Psalm 33:20-21 says, "*We wait in hope for our Lord; He is our help and our shield. In Him our hearts rejoice, for we trust in His holy name.*"

Let us return, for a moment, to the topic of training or teaching our dogs what we want (or do not want) from them. My husband, Jim, and I call ourselves dog trainers; and this is accurate because we train our own dogs to do many things. I compete in rally obedience and agility. Jim competes in agility. But when we work with clients, we are the instructors; they are the trainers. We teach clients how to train their own dogs. Some of our clients also participate in dog sports, such as rally and agility. But many of them simply want a dog that will listen to them and obey them. Believe it or not, a dog is much happier if you take the lead in your relationship with him and teach him how to behave.

It is amazing to me how many people come for training with their dog saying that the dog is "hard-headed" and just won't listen. But in fact, in about ninety-five percent of these cases, it is the owner who is at fault because he or she has not taken their role as "master" seriously. They tell me that the dog will not "sit" or "come" when told to. I then explain to them that just like a new-born human baby does not understand the English language until we teach the baby what words mean, a dog has no concept of what our commands mean until we show him or her. Once we help dogs to understand what we want, they are usually happy to obey, especially if we use rewards in training. I primarily train with food rewards, but some dogs respond better to toys and play as rewards.

So back to the model of master: God is our master. He loves us and wants what is best for us. We should want to obey Him. He has given us the Bible with all the instructions for how He wants us to live. Second Timothy 3:15-17 tells us, "*All scripture is God-breathed and is useful for teaching, rebuking, correcting, and training in righteousness, so that the servant of God may be thoroughly equipped for every good work.*"

Jesse age five months

Photos by Phyllis Ensley

2

UNCONDITIONAL LOVE

Some people say that dogs are easier to love than people, because dogs don't hold grudges. Most anyone who has ever had a dog as a pet will say that dogs love unconditionally. There may be "bad" days where everything went wrong at work or with one's spouse, and without meaning to, the owner takes out his frustration on the dog. Or, there may be times where one's work/school schedule demands much of his or her time, barely leaving any time to spend with his or her dog. But the dog still loves the person and is glad to see him or her.

A much sadder example is an owner who deliberately mistreats his dog. Some examples of this include:

- Chaining or tying the dog outside routinely for long periods of time
- Hitting, kicking, or otherwise physically abusing the dog

🐕 Keeping the dog confined to a crate all the time. Note, there is nothing wrong with crating dogs at night or for other specified times as needed, but not *all* the time.

🐕 Withholding food and/or water for extended periods of time because the dog was "a bad dog."

Even dogs who live in these sad conditions will usually love their owners. If the abuse is severe enough and goes on too long, the dog may try to escape in order to survive. But for the most part, dogs love their owners unconditionally.

So, what does it mean to love unconditionally? It essentially means to love with no strings attached. People are often prone to love someone who is physically attractive, who lives up to certain expectations, earns a good salary, etc. Even wedding vows include the lines "for richer or poorer" and "in sickness and in health." But all too often, a person may leave her spouse if he loses the good- paying job, or a husband may leave his wife after she is diagnosed with a chronic disease. That, of course, is conditional love. To love others unconditionally is sometimes a hard concept to grasp, and even harder to put into practice in everyday life. We often have difficulty loving others this way. The natural thing for people is to love those who treat them well and are kind to them. We have a hard time loving people who mistreat us. Sometimes we have difficulty loving people who do things we don't approve of or who always appear to act selfishly. Some people find it difficult to love those of differing cultural or religious backgrounds.

Dogs illustrate unconditional love toward their owners by loving them no matter how much they are yelled at or ignored by them. Even on days when I spend very little time with my dogs, they are very eager to see me when I come home. They shower me with love. Dogs love their owners, even selfish ones.

God loves us all unconditionally. He loves us on our good days as much as He loves us on our bad days. He loves us when we can feel His love, and He loves us when we don't feel His love. Nothing we can do will make God stop loving us. We may grieve God or cause Him sadness or disappointment. Or, we may cause Him to smile. But either way, He loves us.

I don't think dogs have a concept of forgiveness as we know it. They just love us no matter what we do. Likewise, God loves us no matter what we do. But God does recognize sin, and He wants to forgive us of our sins. God loves us so much that He sent His only Son, Jesus, to die for our sins, so that we could be forgiven. John 3:16 says, "*For God so loved the world that He gave His one and only Son, that whoever believes in Him shall not perish but have eternal life.*"

Jesus suffered and died as the ultimate sacrifice for our sin. Romans 5:8 tells us, "*God demonstrates His own love for us in this: While we were still sinners,*

Christ died for us." And 1 Peter 3:18-19 tells us, "*For Christ also suffered once for sins, the righteous for the unrighteous, to bring you to God. He was put to death in the body but made alive in the Spirit.*"

But the good news is that He was raised from the dead on the third day. We are told in Mark 16:1-6:

> *When the Sabbath was over, Mary Magdalene, Mary the mother of James, and Salome bought spices so that they might go anoint Jesus' body. Very early on the first day of the week, just after sunrise, they were on their way to the tomb and they asked each other, 'Who will roll the stone away from the entrance of the tomb?' But when they looked up, they saw that the stone, which was very large, had been rolled away. As they entered the tomb, they saw a young man, dressed in a white robe sitting on the right side, and they were alarmed. "Don't be alarmed," he said. "You are looking for Jesus the Nazarene who was crucified. He has risen! See the place where they laid him.*"

Then we read that Jesus appeared to His disciples in Luke 24:36-48,

> *...Jesus himself stood among them and said to them, "Peace be with you." They*

were startled and frightened, thinking they saw a ghost. He said to them, "Why are you troubled, and why do doubts rise in your minds? Look at my hands and feet. It is I myself! Touch me and see me; a ghost does not have flesh and bones, as you see I have." When he had said this, he showed them his hands and feet. And while they still did not believe it because of joy and amazement, he asked them, "Do you have anything here to eat?" They gave him a piece of broiled fish, and he took it and ate it in their presence. He said to them, "This is what I told you while I was still with you: Everything must be fulfilled that is written about me in the Law of Moses, the Prophets, and the Psalms." Then he opened their minds so they could understand the scriptures. He told them, "This is what is written: The Messiah will suffer and rise from the dead on the third day, and repentance for the forgiveness of sins will be preached in his name to all nations, beginning at Jerusalem. You are witnesses of these things."

Jesus fulfilled scripture and lives eternally at the right hand of God. And because of His death on the cross, and resurrection from the dead, we can be forgiven of our sins by believing in Him, and thus we can also have eternal life.

3
LOVE EVERYONE

I have heard or read about examples of animals showing love to animals of a different species. Here are a few of them:

Jim and I have a friend named Mark, who used to be one of our pastors at church. He told me the story of a basset hound that his family owned when he was a child. There was a cat in the neighborhood that had kittens. The mother had apparently been hit by a car, although the kittens were weaned. As it was getting chilly in the fall, the kittens came to Mark's family's porch. Their dog welcomed the kittens, who happily snuggled against him to keep warm!

This is such a good lesson for us to learn. We should love people, no matter what color their skin is, no matter what language they speak, and no matter what, if any, is their religion. To love and accept someone does not mean that we agree with everything they say or believe or do. A dog who protects kittens does not start thinking he is a cat. Rather, he is showing love and kindness.

A similar story was about a King Charles spaniel in England who discovered a litter of orphaned baby rabbits. She adopted the baby bunnies and tried to nurse them. She slept with them and protected them.

Another story I read was about a cat (the book is about dogs, but just a little digression). This cat, who happened to have a litter of kittens, found a baby squirrel that had fallen from a tree. She picked him up and took him to her bed with her kittens. She became protective of him and raised him with her own litter of kittens!

Another example (which is not so profound) is the following: A sheltie breeder had two different litters (from two different mothers) at approximately the same time. One of the mothers was unable or unwilling to nurse her puppies. But the mother of the other litter let those puppies come to her and be nursed! Although, in this case, they were the same species, this mother dog had her own puppies to care for and yet took on the additional burden of nursing puppies from the other litter as well. This reminds me of people who adopt children or take in foster children. Children who have no parents or whose parents are unable/unwilling to be parents need the love of someone else.

The stories of animal mothers adopting infants of another species demonstrate how we should love others. For instance, people who adopt children or take in foster children who desperately need

consistent love show us that love includes acceptance of those who are different. (I have several
friends who have adopted children from other
countries, including Russia.) But even if you are not
so inclined to adopt children, there are many ways
to show love and acceptance to people who are
different. Some ways to show love to others include:

- smiling at them instead of looking the other way;
- giving food or clothing to those who need assistance;
- teaching English to someone in this country who speaks a different language;
- remembering that we are all created by God and He wants us to love them the way He loves them.

We have a friend, Meredith, who breeds
Weimaraners (dogs). She and her husband, Bill, also
own and operate a small farm where they raise
chickens, ducks, and lambs, along with an occa-
sional pig. Weimaraners are bred to be used in
hunting birds, but Meredith had one named Elle
who was different. She was very kind to the chickens,
sharing her food with them and never chasing them.
We can really learn from Elle. Often, there are people
who are brought up by their parents, or sad to say
even taught in their church, to hate certain groups
of people of another religion or a different race. But
we are taught in the Bible to love everyone.

We are commanded by God to love the Lord your God with all your heart, with all your soul, with all your strength, and with all your mind, and to love your neighbor as yourself (Lk. 10:27). The parable of the good Samaritan in Luke 10:29-37 addresses this issue. An expert in the law was trying to justify himself, so he asked Jesus, "*And who is my neighbor?*" Jesus told the parable of a man traveling from Jerusalem to Jericho who was attacked by robbers, beaten, and left half dead. There was a priest going down the road who saw the man but avoided him, going to the other side of the road. Then a Levite, traveling the same road, also passed on the other side of the road without stopping to help him. But a Samaritan, traveling down this road, saw the man and took pity on him. He treated the man's wounds, put him on his own donkey and brought him to an inn, and took care of him. The next day, before leaving, he paid the innkeeper to let the man stay there until he was well enough to travel. In Luke 10:36, Jesus asked the expert, "*Which of these three do you think was a neighbor to the man who fell into the hands of robbers?*" The expert in the law replied in verse 37, "*the one who had mercy on him.*" Jesus told him, "*Go and do likewise.*"

4

OBEDIENCE

When we want a dog to obey certain commands, we must teach him or her the words for the actions we want. This means from something as simple as "sit" to complex activities such as competition obedience or agility. If our commands are clear and concise, the dog will more likely be able to follow and obey them. Some dog owners say their dogs are "stupid" or "stubborn" or don't know anything. That responsibility to teach them falls back to the owner, who is the master. If the owner will take time and patience to teach the dog, the dog can and will learn.

Many people say that the Bible is confusing or out of date, but this is not the case. In Hebrews 4:12, we are told, *"For the word of God is alive and active. Sharper than any double-edged sword, it penetrates even to dividing soul and spirit, joints and marrow; it judges the thoughts and attitudes of the heart."* The "word of God" in this verse refers to the

Bible. The words in the Bible were spoken from God to the men who wrote them down for us. Second Timothy 3:16-17 says, "*All Scripture is God-breathed and is useful for teaching, rebuking, correcting, and training in righteousness, so that the servant of God may be thoroughly equipped for every good work.*"

Just as we need to teach our dogs what we expect of them, God has given us clear instructions in the Bible about how we are saved and how we are to live. Although a dog in competitive obedience or other sports may "earn" titles, we do not "earn" our salvation. As described in an earlier chapter in this book, Jesus died on the cross so that our sins could be forgiven. He was resurrected to life on the third day, so that we can have an eternal relationship with Him.

My Belgian Tervuren, Jackson, loves to work for me, whether in rally obedience or agility. His love for working with me and obeying my commands gives me a picture of how we should love to spend time with God and obey His commands. Sometimes dogs want to be "master" instead of submitting to their owners. Jackson is a dog who by nature is not only dominant but also somewhat aggressive, so I have had to work with him from the time he was quite young on exercises such as "nothing in life is free." I had to hand feed him all his meals for several months. This was all done so that he could learn that I am his master. Once that was established, we not only had a better relationship, but he knew who was in control and that he should look to me for direction.

In a similar way, people often do not want to submit to Christ. But He is a loving Master who wants the very best for us, just as we want the best for our dogs. We are the dog's master and friend. Christ is our Master and friend.

Jackson's love of working with me and carrying out my commands brings me great joy. Likewise, when we spend time with God in Bible study and prayer, and live for Him, it brings Him great joy.

When teaching a dog new, desirable behavior, we use rewards in the form of food treats or toys (e.g., a quick game of tug) when they get it right. This is a strong motivator for dogs to do the right thing. After enough repetition, the rewards can be slowly faded away. However, we can always praise the dog for desirable behavior, even after he knows it well enough to perform without food or toy rewards. Then, we can still use rewards occasionally to keep the dog happily performing the behaviors we like.

On the other hand, once a dog knows a behavior well but refuses to do it, this may require correction, or discipline. Discipline, although unpleasant at the time, is a necessary part of love. Discipline that comes with love is difficult for both the master and the recipient of the correction. The correction from a person to a dog should usually be verbal only. A stern, or sometimes even harsh, verbal correction lets the dog know she was wrong and should not repeat the behavior. Just as a parent who loves his/her child will discipline a child when appropriate, so will the dog owner discipline his or her dog. (I do not use any harsh, physical punishment. It is primarily verbal.) If verbal correction is not enough to make the dog understand, I recommend the use of "time-out," much the same as making a child stand in the corner. The time-out must be immediately following the bad behavior. It requires putting the dog in an isolated area, such as a bathroom or laundry room, away from people and other dogs. Five to ten minutes should be sufficient. However, the time-out may need to be repeated multiple times when dealing with very undesirable behavior, such as biting the owner.

Similarly, God loves us and wants the best for us. He expects us to obey His commands in His written word, the Bible. God sometimes disciplines us because He loves us. We are told in Proverbs 3:11-12, *"My son, do not despise the Lord's discipline, and do not resent His rebuke, because the Lord disciplines those He loves, as a father the son he delights in."* It grieves God when we deliberately disobey His commands. Like we want our dog to obey us, He wants us to obey Him.

Jackson age eight months
Photos by Alleyne Dickens

Jackson age two years
Photo by Phyllis Ensley

5

LOYALTY/DEVOTION

Perhaps the most special dog I have ever owned was a Belgian Tervuren named Faith. She was extremely loyal and eager to please me. I got her as a young puppy and had her until she died just shy of fifteen years old. She loved me so much and wanted to please me in everything she did. There arc some animal behaviorists who claim that dogs do not have an innate sense of wanting to please, but rather, the dog just works for rewards or absence of punishment. Although this is true of some dogs, I have definitely seen other dogs who want more than anything to please their owners. Faith was a perfect example of this.

Don't get me wrong: Faith loved getting food treats as rewards for performing well for me in agility. She loved to play with tennis balls and she loved for me to throw a frisbee for her to catch. But the difference is that she wanted to do agility for me and with me. She wanted to play with tennis balls or frisbees with me. It was as though her whole purpose in life was to please me. She loved being with me and she loved my attention. It did not matter whether the attention was training/competing in agility, or whether it was playing frisbee, or snuggling on the sofa.

Faith loved me (her master), and she had her priorities right. Matthew 6:24 tells us, *"No one can serve two masters. Either you will hate the one and love the other, or you will be devoted to the one and despise the other. You cannot serve both God and money."* In this particular verse, it refers to money, which is a huge distraction for many people, but it could be anything to which you are more devoted than to the Lord, God. It could be your job, your hobby, your spouse, etc. Paul says in 2 Corinthians 11:3, *"But I am concerned that just as Eve was deceived by the serpent's cunning, your minds may somehow be led astray from your sincere and pure devotion to Christ."*

So about now, you may be asking me what does this teach us about God's love or how He wants my relationship with Him to be? God loves us so much that He sent His only Son into the world to be born of a virgin, live as a human for about thirty-three years, then to be crucified so that our sins could be forgiven. Jesus never sinned or did anything wrong. But He suffered and died for us, so that if we believe in Him and repent of our sins, He will forgive us and give us an eternal relationship with Him. But He wants our whole hearts, not just to say that we believe in Him. Jesus told us in Matthew 22:37-39, *"Love the Lord your God with all your heart, and with all your soul and with all your mind. This is the first and greatest commandment. And the second is like it: Love your neighbor as yourself.*" My dog Faith loved me with all her heart and mind. Her love for me was a perfect example of how God wants us to love Him.

A friend of mine, Carrole, has a dog named Gilda. Gilda loves Carrole very much. She likes Carrole's sister, niece, and brother, whom she sees often, and she likes me. But she does not love us the way she loves Carrole. Carrole lives with her brother and niece. Gilda will obey them when Carrole is not home, but if Carrole is home, Gilda is totally devoted to her and does not pay much attention to the others. That is the type of devotion that God wants us to have toward Him. He never leaves us though. He wants us to have friends and love other people, but He wants us to love Him more than anyone or anything else.

On another note, dogs are pack animals. They want to be part of a pack, or part of the family. Dogs are not happy when they are left outside all the time or when they receive no attention from the people they live with. Whether it is going for walks with us or laying at our feet in the house, they want to be near us. They can't wait for us to come home from work so that they can see us and be with us. This is how God wants us to be with our church family. We go to church services to worship God, but He also wants us to long to be together the way our dogs long to be with us. In the New Testament, the early Christians were referred to as brothers and sisters; that is the way we should still see each other today.

Faith age fifteen years
Photo by Phyllis Ensley

Faith age fifteen years
Photo by Carole Corbin

6

STAY/WAIT

You've probably heard the expression, "Good things come to those who wait." This can also be true for dogs. If you who have ever competed in the sport of dog agility, you have likely also heard the expression, "No stay, no play." For those of you who have never done agility with a dog, the reasoning behind this statement is that the dog needs to "stay" or "wait" at the start line for the handler to lead out past the first one or two obstacles. If the dog breaks its stay, the handler may be doomed for the entire course. This is especially important for dogs that run much faster than the handler. I've got one of those now! The dog who does wait on the start line until the handler releases him gets to run the agility course and then gets a reward (good things come to those who wait).

Teaching a dog to stay is challenging for the average dog owner. There are two reasons for this. The obvious one that most people think about is that the dog wants to get up and do something more fun. But the primary reason is that the owner/trainer does not have the patience to correctly teach a dog what the "stay" command means. If you simply tell a dog to stay and immediately walk away, the chances are the dog will follow you, because he has no idea what the word "stay" means. Therefore, it is the responsibility of the person to teach the dog what it means and what he or she expects of the dog. There should be lots of rewards and praise for staying, with a verbal correction and absence of reward for breaking the stay. I mentioned patience above because the trainer needs to start with two seconds and very gradually work up to longer periods of time. He or she should also stay with the dog initially, and then very gradually increase the distance he or she walks away from the dog.

I explained the process in detail because it is often the people who are the most impatient (even more so than dogs, except young puppies). Teaching a dog to "stay" (or "wait") requires a lot of patiently "waiting" on the owner's part. You should wait until the dog can stay in place for two to three seconds before trying to increase the amount of time you expect him or her to stay. Wait until the dog can reliably stay for ten to fifteen seconds before taking one-two steps away from the dog. Continue the training, increasing the amount of time to ten to fifteen seconds before you lengthen your distance from the dog.

It can be important to you for your dog to learn and obey the "stay/wait" command. It is also important for people to learn to *wait* on God. The Bible tells us in Psalm 130:5, "*I wait for the Lord, my whole being waits, and in His word, I put my hope.*" Psalm 27:14 says, "*Wait for the Lord; be strong and take heart and wait for the Lord.*" You may wonder, "What are we waiting for from God?" This can be a number of different things.

First, I think about waiting on God to answer our prayers. We are told in the Bible that if we ask God for anything that is in accordance with His will, He will answer. But sometimes God's timing is very different from our timing. We must pray in faith, knowing that He will answer our prayers when He thinks it's the appropriate time. It is a matter of patiently waiting for God to answer our prayers.

Secondly, we may need to wait for God to rescue us from difficult situations, such as illness, job difficulties, or problems in a relationship. Psalm 40:1-3 talks about how David waited patiently for the Lord, and He rescued David from physical harm as well as depression.

At the time I am writing this, we are experiencing the coronavirus pandemic. Many people are fearful about the possibility of illness or death. Some are fearful about the economy, due to the dramatic drops in the stock market and the fact that so many people are temporarily unemployed due to the pandemic. Some people are simply depressed because they are required to stay at home and cannot participate in their normal activities. It is a difficult time for everyone, but our hope is in the Lord Jesus Christ. The Bible says in Isaiah 30:18, "*Yet the Lord longs to be gracious to you; therefore, He will rise up to show you compassion. For the Lord is a God of justice. Blessed are all who wait for Him.*"

This is the most important reason we should wait on the Lord. We are told the following in Titus 2:11-13:

> *For the grace of God has appeared that offers salvation to all people. It teaches us to say "no" to ungodliness and worldly passions, and to live self-controlled, upright and godly lives in this present age, while we wait for the blessed hope – the appearing of our great God and Savior, Jesus Christ.*

This scripture mentions *waiting* for the blessed hope, which is the appearing of our Savior, Jesus Christ. What does this mean to you and me? It is referring to the Second Coming of Jesus Christ, including the resurrection of Christians to reign with Him in glory.

No matter what you may be experiencing right now, none if it compares to the promise that is given to Christians – the promise of eternal life, with bodies that experience no more pain or sorrow. In Philippians 3:20-21, we are told:

But our citizenship is in heaven. And we eagerly await a Savior from there, the Lord Jesus Christ, who, by the power that enables him to bring everything under His control, will transform our lowly bodies so that they will be like His glorious body.

As you can see, learning to wait on God offers the greatest reward of all.

7

BITS AND KIBBLE

Bad Company Corrupts Good Character

Our friend Mark had a basset hound that was kind and gentle toward some kittens. They would come and snuggle against the dog to keep warm. But one day, something terrible happened. A dog from next door came over and started attacking the kittens. Then Mark's dog joined in and helped the other dog kill the kittens! I have heard from a canine behavior expert that a dog who is typically not aggressive will join in when another dog starts to attack someone or something. The Bible tells us in 1 Corinthians 15:33, *"Do not be misled: 'Bad company corrupts good character.'"* One example of this for people is when a person begins to poke fun at another person, and then other people join in. On a more serious note, when a teenager starts "hanging out" with someone who does drugs, he may be tempted or even feel pressured to copy the behavior.

Living in the Present

Dogs do not typically sit around worrying about what they are going to do tomorrow or what they will wear. They do not even worry about the weather (unless there is a thunderstorm). Neither do dogs have financial worries or aspirations to "get ahead." They enjoy the present moment and make the most of it. Whether it is a romp in the woods, chasing a tennis ball, or snuggling next to their favorite human, they tend to be content with the present time. We are told in Matthew 6:33-34, *"But seek first His kingdom and His righteousness, and all these things will be given to you as well. Therefore, do not worry about tomorrow, for tomorrow will worry about itself."*

Follow Me

I have a friend named Nicki who has a chocolate Lab named Ace. She told me that she sometimes goes out on her four-wheeler and lets Ace run along beside it for exercise. Sometimes he would get distracted by something in the woods and start to wander off. Then Nicki would call Ace and say, "Follow me." Ace would come back and run alongside her again. But after a while, he would start to wander again. So then again, she would tell Ace, "Follow me," and again he would come back and run alongside her. In Matthew 16:24, Jesus told His disciples, *"Whoever wants to be my disciple must deny themselves and take up their cross and follow me."* In our Christian walk, sometimes the Holy Spirit prompts us when we start to wander and reminds us to follow Christ.

Can We Do the Impossible?

Our dogs often look to us to do what is impossible for them. Sometimes it is something that is also impossible for humans. A friend of mine used to have an Australian cattle dog named Foxy Kay. One particular winter, we got a lot more snow than is usual for Virginia. As soon as the snow would start to melt, we would get another big snowfall. Foxy Kay was a very intelligent dog who did not like to go out in the snow. Carrie's dog looked at the snow, looked at her, looked back at the snow, and then fixed her gaze on Carrie, as if to ask, "Can't you make this stuff go away?" Even though we sometimes seem like a "god" to our dogs, we are not all powerful as is our almighty God. God is able to do what seems impossible to us. Ephesians 3:20-21 says, *"Now to Him who is able to do immeasurably more than all we ask or imagine, according to His power that is at work within us, to Him be glory in the church and in Christ Jesus throughout all generations, forever and ever!"*

Puppies Learn from Older Dogs

If you've ever purchased a puppy when you already have an adult dog, you may have noticed that some behaviors are easier to teach the new pup. An example of this is potty training. You still need to take the puppy outside frequently and praise him/her for doing his/her business outside. And you need to watch the pup inside the house so that if he/she gets ready to potty in the house, you quickly take him/her outside. But the beautiful thing is that you can take your puppy and adult dog outside together. When the pup sees the other dog "go potty" outdoors, rather than in the house, he/she is likely to follow the example of the adult dog. Another example is feeding time. I like for my dogs to sit and "stay" for about fifteen seconds before I release them to go eat their meal. Although it takes a little while to teach a puppy what the "stay" command means, he/she will likely watch the older dog(s) and learn this more quickly by following their example. Just as an older dog may help us teach a younger one, Jesus commanded Christians to teach younger Christians. He says in Matthew 28:19-20, "*Therefore go and make disciples of all nations, baptizing them in the name of the Father and the Son and of the Holy Spirit, and teaching them to obey everything I have commanded you.*"

Charlie and Jesse
Photo by Phyllis Ensley

Part 2

LESSONS TAUGHT BY SPECIFIC TYPES OF DOGS

8
FEARFUL DOGS

We have a twelve-year-old sheltie named Charlie. Charlie is very beautiful and exceptionally smart. He was very good at the sport of agility when he was young; but when he was about three years old, something went wrong. He became extremely fearful. We consulted with an animal communicator and veterinarians. The consensus was that he is exceptionally sound sensitive, and there is nothing we can do other than give him medication to treat anxiety. Even with medication, his fearfulness seemed to get worse over the next two to three years. We had done the recommended socializing with him as a puppy and he had been fine.

Needless to say, we had to stop Charlie's agility career by the time he was five years old. He would be running an agility course beautifully, but then, somewhere in the distance, somebody would slam a door. Charlie would literally become frozen by fear. In addition, he would be so terrified in a hotel room that he would try to hide under the bed or a large piece of furniture. We tried different medications to help him, but even though they took some of the edge off his fear, he was still miserable. It broke my heart to see him literally suffering from the fear and anxiety. Perhaps the saddest part of this story is that he loved the sport of agility!

Even after we stopped taking Charlie to agility trials, he still suffered from fear; he still suffers to this day. We would try to take him for walks down the street, but he could hear cows or other noises that terrified him and he literally could not walk down the street any longer. He seems to be fine most of the time in the house and in our yard. But even in the yard, if he hears gun shots a mile or more away, he freaks and tries to run from the noise. We have done everything we can to help Charlie have a good quality of life, but we can never take away the sound sensitivity that plagues him.

Similarly, my friend Carrole has a Belgian Tervuren named Win who is quite fearful. There is a difference though. Whereas Charlie's fear stems from noise, Win is more frightened by sights. When Win was a puppy, I went with Carrole to a number of places to get him acclimated to different sights and sounds and people. While he typically loves people, and some sounds frighten him, Win is most fearful of things that look unfamiliar and things that move in the wind. Like Charlie, Win's fear seemed to escalate as he got older. Win is four years old now and we continue to work with him. Again, I want to emphasize that both

Win and Charlie were socialized and introduced to various stimuli from the time they were puppies. They were given treat rewards and/or toy rewards when introduced to "scary" or unusual things. In both cases, they were fine as puppies and young adults, but the fears became more pronounced as they got older.

So, where am I going with all this? People, like dogs have, fears and anxieties. Some are more prone to anxiety than others. And people, like dogs, sometimes may need medication to help them deal with anxiety. However, most fear and anxiety that people experience can be conquered by learning how to turn it over to God and trust Him.

The Bible speaks about two different kinds of fear. The first one is the fear of God. For example, 1 Samuel 12:24 says, *"But be sure to fear the Lord and serve Him faithfully with all your heart; consider what great things He has done for you."* Psalm 111:10 says, *"The fear of the Lord is the beginning of wisdom; all who follow His precepts have good understanding. To Him belongs eternal praise."* In Proverbs 1:7, we are told, *"The fear of the Lord is the beginning of knowledge, but fools despise wisdom and instruction."* The fear of God in these verses means to have a reverent awe for God and submit to Him. This is the kind of fear that God wants us to have.

The other type of fear is fear of the unknown, fear of bad things happening, or perhaps fear of another person. This is the type of fear that accompanies anxiety. God did give us a brain, so He expects us to use it to keep ourselves out of harm's way whenever possible. That being said, if we are fearful about the future or afraid of the unknown, there is nothing we can humanly do about these types of anxiety. But God can do what is humanly impossible. Psalm 34:4 tells us, "*I sought the Lord, and He answered me; He delivered me from all my fears.*" We are told in 1 Peter 5:6-7, "*Humble yourselves, therefore, under God's mighty hand, that He may lift you up in due time. Cast all your anxiety on Him because He cares for you.*" These verses show us that God, in His infinite power and love, can and will deliver us from our fears if we go to Him.

One of my favorite verses in the entire Bible is Philippians 4:6-7. It says:

> *Do not be anxious about anything, but in every situation, by prayer and petition, with thanksgiving, present your requests to God. And the peace of God which transcends all understanding, will guard your hearts and your minds in Christ Jesus.*

This verse tells us how to turn our fears and anxiety over to God. We are told to pray, with thanksgiving, presenting our requests to God. I have seen this work in my life numerous times; it will work for you too.

We are currently experiencing the coronavirus pandemic. More and more people are becoming ill every day. More people are dying. The stock market has dropped astronomically. Many people are out of work due to the imposed quarantine. People are afraid: afraid of getting sick; afraid of losing all their savings; afraid the world may be coming to an end. This is definitely a difficult time for everyone. But I believe Psalm 23 speaks to this fear so beautifully. Psalm 23:1-4 says:

> *The Lord is my shepherd, I lack nothing. He makes me lie down in green pastures, he leads me beside quiet waters, He refreshes my soul. He guides me along the right paths for His name's sake. Even though I walk through the darkest valley, I will fear no evil, for You are with me; your rod and your staff, they comfort me.*

This tells us that even when we are experiencing dark, perilous times, we do not need to fear. The first verse refers to the Lord as our shepherd. At the end of verse 4, it mentions His rod and staff. These were tools that shepherds used to protect and direct the sheep. Likewise, the Lord will protect and direct us if we ask Him and give our anxiety to Him.

In the case of dogs, we humans are the masters or shepherds who do everything we can to keep our dogs safe and free of fear. There is a major difference in this analogy because we, being human, cannot always take away a dog's fears. But God can give us peace, even in difficult times such as we are experiencing now. He goes a step further in 1 John 4:18-19 to say, "*There is no fear in love. But perfect love drives out fear, because fear has to do with punishment. The one who fears is not made perfect in love. We love because He first loved us.*" In other words, once we understand God's love for us, along with His amazing power, we no longer need to fear things such as illness or even death. Once we have a relationship with God through Jesus Christ, we can be assured of our place with Him in heaven for all eternity.

Charlie age six years
Photo by Phyllis Ensley

9
PERFORMANCE DOGS

Many of my friends have what are called "performance" dogs. These are typically dogs that were bred to excel in certain sports, such as agility, herding, flyball, and obedience. Other dogs are bred to excel in conformation. And, of course, the majority of dogs are simply beloved pets. Some breeders attempt to breed dogs which excel in all these areas. Performance dogs can also make good pets. Sometimes dogs who were bred to be pets also become excellent performance dogs.

Many people who have performance dogs show in one or more of the above sports and/or rally, scent work, barn hunt, and dock diving. The majority of people who participate in any of these sports do so because they enjoy training and showing their dogs. And they often participate in these activities because that is where they see their friends.

My husband, Jim, and I enjoy competing in the sport of dog agility. This entails a handler with his/her dog, running the dog through an obstacle course. The course consists of jumps, tunnels, weave poles, and contact obstacles. The handler runs with his/her dog, giving the dog cues along the way, directing him/her which obstacles to take. In a given class and jump height, the dog who completes the course flawlessly with the fastest time is the winner. My first agility dog was a sheltie named Forest. Forest ran very fast, and once I learned how to handle him, he won a lot of blue ribbons.`

Most people like to win. Whether dog agility, soccer, football, or even a school science fair, people like to win or be on the winning team. NFL players love to go to the Super Bowl, and they love to win the Super Bowl. Even for the general public, who simply watch football games on television, we like to see our favorite teams win.

As I mentioned above, there are different reasons why people participate in dog sports. It may be primarily to spend time with their dogs, or to make friends who share a common interest. However, there are also a lot of people who play to win. But winning may mean different things to different people. To some, it is winning the blue ribbons on individual runs. To some, it is qualifying to compete at the National Agility Championship. To others, it may be to win a national competition; and to others, it may mean earning a place on the United States world agility team. For some, winning means earning titles on their dogs. In AKC agility, many people aspire to earning the title of MACH (Master Agility Champion).

Most of us love to win. In dog sports, we rarely win much, if any, money. But it is the thrill of winning that we aspire to. In agility, when we run a very fast dog, just the thrill of having a "clean run" may be the goal. (A clean run means running the entire course with no faults – no knocked bars, no missed contacts, no off-courses, and no refusals.)

The thrill of winning a competition or an agility championship, while satisfying, is only temporary. Winning the race of living daily for Christ brings joy that lasts forever. First Corinthians 9:24-25 explains it this way:

> *Do you not know that in a race all the runners run, but only one gets the prize? Everyone who competes in the games goes into strict training. They do it to get a crown that will not last, but we do it to get a crown that will last forever.*

A crown that will last refers to eternal life. Philippians 3:14 says, "*I press on toward the goal to win the prize for which God has called me heavenward in Christ Jesus.*" This does not mean that we earn our salvation. We are saved only by the grace of God, through the blood of our Lord Jesus Christ. Rather, it means that once we become a Christian (follower of Christ), we strive to become more like Christ as long as we live here on earth. Heaven will be our long-awaited prize.

Paul, nearing the end of his life on earth, said in 2 Timothy 2:7-8:

> *I have fought the good fight, I have finished the race, I have kept the faith. Now there is in store for me the crown of righteousness, which the Lord, the righteous Judge, will award to me on that day – and not only to me, but to all who have longed for His appearing.*

Photo by Phyllis Ensley

Photo by Ian Stewart

Photo by Ian Stewart

Photo by Ian Stewart

Photo by Ian Stewart

Photo by Ian Stewart

10

RESCUE DOGS

When we rescue a dog from a shelter or a dumpster, we may be rescuing it from physical death or from a life of abuse. My husband and I have rescued three different dogs, and taken on a couple as re-home dogs. We have been fortunate that none of these dogs came with a lot of baggage, in terms of having been abused or mistreated. However, we have worked with both boarding and training clients who have rescued dogs from terrible situations. These dogs often suffer from severe separation anxiety and/or fear aggression.

Hopefully anyone who rescues a dog will give it a loving home and provide for all its needs. Many rescue dogs become very bonded with the new owner once they learn to trust him or her. They often make the best pets.

The first dog Jim and I rescued was a cocker spaniel, whom we named Joshua. Although we did not know how old he was when we got him from the local rescue group, our veterinarian thought Joshua was approximately two years old. We were told by the rescue group that he had already been through three or four homes before they got him. We knew the reason as soon as we evaluated him. He was a dog who, as a youngster, needed a job to do and needed exercise. We started training him for agility and he took to it like a duck to water. He loved to run and jump and was exceptionally fast. We gave him the perfect home where he had lots of attention as well as exercise and stimulation. We still have Joshua, who is now at least sixteen years old.

We have another rescue dog, Emmy Lou. She is thought to be half border collie and half Australian cattle dog. We were fortunate enough to get her as a puppy from a herding dog rescue group in Richmond, Virginia. Although Emmy Lou does not particularly like to do agility, she adores Jim and he takes her everywhere with him. Although many people say they like Australian cattle dogs, the truth is they can be very hard to live with unless they are in the right environment where, again, they receive a lot of attention, stimulation, and exercise. The same is true of border collies. By the way, Emmy Lou's favorite activity is hiking, and Jim usually takes her hiking at least twice a week.

There are hundreds of similar stories from other people who have rescued dogs. Many of these dogs excel in competitive dog sports, while others are simply loyal, loving pets. The main point is that a large number of these dogs were rescued from some sort of suffering or even death.

Humans also need to be rescued; we need rescuing from sin and death. You may be saying to yourself, "I'm not that bad." But every one of us has sinned. We read in Romans 3:23, "*for all have sinned and fall short of the glory of God.*" Christ died on the cross so that we could be saved from spiritual death and born into new lives. Romans 5:8 tells us: "*But God demonstrates His own love for us in this: While we were still sinners, Christ died for us.*"

He suffered and died so that we could be saved. But the best news is that Christ did not remain dead. He was raised on the third day and now lives forever. He is the Son of God, and He will rescue us from our sins. When we believe in Him, confess our sins, and turn to Him, He forgives us and gives us new life. We will then have an eternal relationship with Him.

Just as a dog cannot rescue itself, we cannot rescue ourselves. Ephesians 2:8-9 tells us: "*For it is by grace you have been saved, through faith – not by works, so that no one can boast.*" In other words, we cannot earn our salvation. We are saved by grace, through faith in our Lord Jesus Christ.

Joshua age seven years
photo by Ian Stewart

Emmy Lou age two years
photo by Phyllis Ensley

Part 3

CONCLUSION

11

BOUGHT AT A PRICE

When we get a dog, we usually have to pay a price for it. This can be anywhere from $100 to $2000 (or more). Some people may pay as much as $5000 to purchase the dog they want. Even rescue dogs, that we get from a shelter or rescue group, may cost up to $250. Once we purchase a dog, it belongs to us.

There are essentially two things that make something valuable:

1)   Who made it?
2)   What will someone pay for it?

We, as humans, are extremely valuable. God created us. And the ultimate price was paid for us, for our salvation, when Jesus died on the cross. Jesus paid the ultimate price for us. He gave His life for us so that we could be forgiven of our sins and have a relationship with Him. We are told in 1 Peter 1:18-19:

For you know that it was not with perishable things such as silver or gold that you were redeemed from the empty way of life handed down to you from your ancestors, but with the precious blood of Christ, a lamb without blemish or defect.

When we come to believe in Him, ask Him to forgive our sins, and make a decision to follow Him, He forgives us, He saves us, and He gives us eternal life. In other words, when we give our lives to Him, we become His. We belong to Him. First Corinthians 6:19-20 says, "*Do you not know that your bodies are temples of the Holy Spirit, who is in you, whom you have received from God? You are not your own; you were bought at a price. Therefore, honor God with your bodies.*"

How do you know if you belong to Christ? In other words, how do you know if you are saved? Do you know for certain that you have eternal life? First and foremost, you must be born again. In John 3:3, we are told, "*Jesus replied, 'Very truly I tell you, no one can enter the kingdom of God unless they are born again.'*"

You then might ask, "How can I be born again?" First, you must believe in the Lord Jesus Christ. To believe in Him includes the following:

🐕 Believe that He was born of a virgin, conceived by the Holy Spirit.

- Believe that He lived on earth as a sinless man, healing the sick and lame, and teaching about the Kingdom of God.
- Believe that He was crucified – His blood was shed for our sins.
- Believe that He arose from the dead on the third day.
- Believe that He is the Son of God, and the only way to God is through a relationship with Jesus Christ.
- Believe that He is your Lord and Master.

Once you believe in Him, you must confess that Jesus Christ is your Lord. Romans 10:9 tells us, "*If you declare with your mouth, 'Jesus is Lord,' and believe in your heart that God raised Him from the dead, you will be saved.*" When you become a Christian, you become a disciple, or follower, of Christ. The next step to salvation is repentance. This means being truly sorry for your sins, and then turning away from sin. Second Corinthians 7:10 says, "*Godly sorrow brings repentance that leads to salvation.*" We are also told in Acts 2:38, "*Repent and be baptized, every one of you for the forgiveness of your sins. And you will receive the gift of the Holy Spirit.*" Once you believe that Jesus is Lord, confess that with your lips, and repent of your sins, you are born again. This is when you are saved and receive the heart-changing gift of the Holy Spirit.

When a person is truly saved, or born again, he recognizes that he must completely surrender his life to the lordship of Jesus Christ. Jesus told us in Matthew 16:24, "*Whoever wants to be my disciple must deny themselves and take up their cross and follow me.*"

The Bible tells us in 2 Corinthians 5:17, "*Therefore, if anyone is in Christ, the new creation has come: The old has gone, the new is here!*" In other words, when we become a Christian, a follower of Christ, our lives will change.

A person who belongs to Christ will show it by the way he lives. Jesus said in Matthew 7:16-20:

> *By their fruit you will recognize them. Do people pick grapes from thorn-bushes, or figs from thistles? Likewise, every good tree bears good fruit, but a bad tree bears bad fruit. Every tree that does not bear good fruit is cut down and thrown into the fire. Thus, by their fruit you will recognize them.*

Once we are saved, we will begin to bear good fruit for the Lord. What is this fruit? Galatians 5:22-23 tells us: "*But the fruit of the Spirit is love, joy, peace, forbearance, kindness, goodness, faithfulness, gentleness, and self-control.*"

In conclusion, I want to reiterate that we are saved by grace, through faith in the Lord Jesus. Ephesians 2:8-9 tells us: "*For it is by grace you have been saved, through faith—and this is not from your-selves, it is the gift of God—not by works, so that no one can boast.*"

When you purchase a dog, it belongs to you; you are its master. Jesus Christ purchased us with His blood. We belong to Him. He is our Master.

Jackson age four months
Photo by Ian Stewart

ABOUT THE AUTHOR

Cindy Rose has been training her own dogs her entire life since the age of ten years. At age ten, on her own, she taught her black Labrador Retriever the basic commands of come, sit, down, stay, and heel, and she also showed him in Junior Showmanship at dog shows, with several placements.

As an adult, her first dog was a Shetland sheepdog (sheltie) and she competed in obedience with him. Her second sheltie, Forest, was her first agility dog. She put numerous obedience and agility titles on him, and they competed at the national level in agility. Cindy assisted and later taught obedience classes for a local dog club.

In 2002, she and her husband Jim launched their own dog training business and boarding kennel. She has put numerous obedience, rally, and agility titles on two Belgian Tervuren and two more shelties.

Working with the public as a dog trainer, Cindy has worked with all types of dogs, including Great Danes, Mastiffs, German shepherds, Labs, Golden Retrievers, Weimaraners, etc., in addition to small dogs such as Dachsunds, Yorkies, and Beagles.

Cindy is actively involved in a local church, where she has taught a women's Sunday School class. She also participates in a weekly in-depth Bible study. She currently does pet therapy visitations with her small sheltie at a local nursing home. At this time, she competes occasionally in rally and agility with her young Belgian Tervuren.